HOW TO HUMANISTICALLY HANDLE BAD BULLYING BOSSES
BY JENNIFER HANCOCK

Published by Jennifer Hancock

Copyright 2020 by Jennifer Hancock

Published 2020

Paperback Edition

Title: How to Humanistically Handle Bad Bullying Bosses

Author: Jennifer Hancock

Editor: Desiree Vogelpohl

ISBN: 9781652011156

Imprint: Independently published

This book is also available as an ebook at most online retailers

All rights reserved. No part of this book may be used or reproduced in any manner whatsoever without written permission, except in the case of brief quotations embodied in critical articles or reviews.

Table of Contents

CHAPTER 1: BULLYING IS NOT A VALID MANAGEMENT TECHNIQUE.. 7

CHAPTER 2: WHAT BULLYING IS – AND IS NOT 9

CHAPTER 3: DEFINING BAD BOSSES 13

CHAPTER 4: WHAT TO DO IF YOUR BOSS IS THE PROBLEM... 17

CHAPTER 5: BEHAVIORAL SCIENCE ON HOW BEHAVIORS ARE LEARNED AND UNLEARNED 23

CHAPTER 6: APPLYING THIS TO YOUR BOSS 27

CHAPTER 7: HOW TO REMOVE REWARDS OR WORK AROUND A BAD BULLYING BOSS 31

CHAPTER 8: WHAT IF THEY ARE REALLY ABUSIVE? 39

CHAPTER 9: THE IMPORTANCE OF DIGNITY 45

CHAPTER 10: HUMANISTIC MANAGEMENT AS AN ALTERNATIVE 47

CHAPTER 11: ABOUT THE AUTHOR 49

CHAPTER 1: BULLYING IS NOT A VALID MANAGEMENT TECHNIQUE

This should not need to be said, but bullying is not a valid management technique. Management by intimidation is managing people with fear. It's not a very effective way to get people to do work. There are other better ways to maintain work levels and increase accountability.

It's also expensive because it encourages fraud and reduces transparency as people start lying to avoid the bosses' ire. This, in turn, negatively impacts decision making – because leaders end up making decisions with bad or inaccurate information.

Finally, it causes negative effects on morale. No one likes working for a bullying boss. No one. It also serves no legitimate purpose. If you ask someone to do some work – you can do that in a variety of ways. It's rare that yelling and putting people down is "necessary" to getting the work done.

What we should all be striving for is workplaces that treat each employee and customer with dignity. This is the ideal of humanistic leadership and management: leading with dignity.

Bullying demeans people, serves no legitimate purpose and should be viewed as not just unnecessary – but counterproductive and it should not be tolerated at all. From anyone, let alone a manager.

~~~~~

CHAPTER 2: WHAT BULLYING IS – AND IS NOT

Let's start by defining what bullying is. First, bullying and harassment are the same thing. Don't treat them as if they are something different. They aren't.

All 50 states define harassment in their criminal codes. This means that harassment is a criminal offense – not just a workplace violation. It is usually considered a misdemeanor but sometimes it is a felony. Treat this as a serious crime and not just as a workplace liability.

Criminal statutes generally **define harassment** as a pattern of behavior that harasses or upsets the target that serves no legitimate purpose. It's that last bit that matters most when we are talking about bullying in the workplace. Does the behavior serve a legitimate purpose?

In the workplace, a manager is going to have repeated behaviors designed to help encourage employees to get work done. It's entirely possible that an employee might feel harassed by this.

Does it serve a legitimate purpose?

But if the behavior serves a legitimate purpose, it would be considered a reasonable management action. When it becomes bullying or harassment is when the behavior is disrespectful, upsetting, AND serves no legitimate purpose. Or if it is unnecessarily aggressive.

For instance, if you ask someone to do some work – you can do that in a variety of ways. It's rare that yelling and putting people down is "necessary" to getting the work done. Yelling is only necessary if you are working in a really loud environment.

Putting someone down, insulting them, or calling them names is never necessary in a work environment and would not serve a legitimate purpose. Anyone who thinks it does is a problem person.

When it comes to bullying, the test is not just that the behavior is unpleasant. The test of whether the behavior crosses the line or not and becomes harassment – is whether it served a legitimate purpose or not.

For instance: if you have a manager who is accused of wrongdoing, you have a legitimate need to investigate them. That manager may view that investigation as a form of harassment because to them it is upsetting. But it's a reasonable and necessary management action. It is impossible to investigate someone without upsetting them a bit. An investigation would not be considered harassment or bullying, unless the investigation served no legitimate purpose. And in case you were wondering, yes there really was a lawsuit where this was determined. Investigating an employee is considered a legitimate management action.

Bullying as a tool of social control

The second aspect of bullying that I want to focus on is that it is used as a tool of social control. This is the reward a bully gets from bullying: control over others through aggression. This is why managers sometimes default to bullying or harassing workers. When we talk about how to control bullying bosses, the concept of social control is going to become important.

For now, understand that a bully uses their aggression to control social groups through strategic inclusion and exclusion. People they don't like are excluded through demeaning comments or other harassing behavior to push them out.

Having a manager that is actively excluding employees through bullying and harassment is bad. Really, really bad. It's morally bad and it is pragmatically bad because it has a negative cascading impact on your business and problem solving in particular.

~~~~~

CHAPTER 3: DEFINING BAD BOSSES

One of the problems we have when dealing with bullying is that the term "bullying" doesn't really mean anything. It could mean anything.

Are they withholding information? Calling people names? Do they have a legitimate mental health problem? Do they require constant positive reinforcement the way a narcissist does? Do they have memory problems? Are they a sociopath or a psychopath?

With the mental health issues, you may not know; and unless you are a doctor, their mental health status is not yours to know. This is why when you are dealing with a bullying boss, it's best to focus on the specific problem behavior and not the reasons it is occurring. Why? Because fixing problem behaviors does not require a mental health diagnosis.

For instance, if they are yelling a lot, that is a behavior that can be addressed through behavioral modification and coaching. If they are not giving employees clear instructions, that is a behavior that can be addressed through training and coaching.

The point is – even if the boss is really, really obnoxious – you can focus on specific behaviors that are inappropriate, unnecessary, and counterproductive to workplace management.

Remember: bullying is a pattern of behavior that serves no legitimate purpose. If a manager doesn't know other more effective ways to manage, that could potentially be fixed with better training.

Whenever I train executive leadership teams, one of the questions I always ask is – "Have you ever promoted a great employee to a management position only to have that employee turn into a jerk?"

Yes?

The reason for that isn't necessarily that the employee is a horrible person. It's more that – they may not know how to manage people. They may never have been taught how to manage the interpersonal issues that are the hallmark of management. Who knows what they think a manager does? Maybe they are trying to emulate a person they saw in a movie.

If you want good managers, train them on how to be good managers and you will lessen the likelihood that your managers will become bad bullying bosses.

Humanistically handling bad bullying bosses means recognizing that the bad bullying boss might not be a bad person. They may just need management training.

~~~~~

CHAPTER 4: WHAT TO DO IF YOUR BOSS IS THE PROBLEM

What should you do if your boss is truly a problem?

It's all very well to be reminded that it's possible that your boss is – you know – human. But if your boss is behaving badly, what do you do?

Well first, Be explicit about what exactly the problem behaviors are. Just saying they are bad doesn't tell me anything. What exactly are they doing that makes them "bad"?

Do they lose their temper? Yell? Eat too loudly during lunches? Punch people? What exactly are they doing that is inappropriate and when does it normally happen?

Keep a documentation log

Start keeping a log of incidences and see if you can identify a pattern of behavior. A good log includes what exactly happened. What exactly was said? When did it happen? Where did it happen? Who was present and witnessed it and Is there any evidence that it happened?

The log serves 2 purposes:

1. It helps you identify the problem behaviors so you can start creating a strategy to deal with it.
2. It provides documentation if the problem is serious and you need to file a formal complaint or if employment action is required.

Humanize Them

The next thing you should do is humanize them so that you can help them behave better. Again – this book is called: *How to Humanistically Handle Bad Bullying Bosses*. Treating everyone we work with – including bad bullying bosses - with dignity is our goal.

How do we humanize them? We consider them compassionately. There are several reasons why humans behave badly.

Are they insecure or anxious?

Sometimes people behave badly because they are insecure or anxious.

Some people handle stress better than others and that impacts how people act in management situations. People who don't respond well to stress, often behave badly.

FOR EXAMPLE:
My husband had a boss that he really liked, but whenever she was anxious – her anxiety spilled all over the place and she became aggressive. It wasn't like her normally – it's just she would get too anxious to be the calm, cool, and collected manager she probably aspired to be and normally was.

Do they have control issues?

Another reason people might behave poorly is because: lack of control. It really stresses some people out. Management is largely about control. It's a job of coordinating the work of other people. Being a manager means being dependent on the work of other people. For people with control issues, being a manager can be incredibly stressful, which can make them anxious. Then we get all the anger management issues that come when people are too anxious to behave well.

This doesn't mean the person is bad – it means they need to learn how to be more calm about things beyond their control. It may also mean that managing other people may not be a good job fit for them.

Are they naturally aggressive?

Another reason some people act poorly is because they are naturally aggressive and they have learned throughout their lives that if they want someone to do something, they get more aggressive and magically – the other person backs down and does what they want them to do.

In other words, somewhere along the way – they learned that bullying people works and so they bully to get what they want. This is the epitome of a bad bullying boss. They bully strategically because it works. They can be trained to stop. But it isn't easy to do. It can be done – it just may be REALLY hard to do.

Do they have a dark triad personality disorder?

Finally, some people behave badly because they have a dark triad personality disorder. Someone who suffers from Narcissism, Machiavellianism, or Psychopathy will behave badly because they can't really help themselves. Their brains are different from other people and it can be seen in brain scans.

All three of the dark triad personality traits have strong genetic components.

Dark Triad Personality Disorders are something someone suffers from. Again – compassion and dignity for the problem individual is important. This doesn't mean you should let them hurt people in the workplace. It just means that it should help inform how you deal with it. In other words: with compassion.

The good news is that only about 1% of the population has psychopathy. Only about 1% suffer from Narcissism and only about 4% suffer from sociopathy. It is rare that you will come across this.

Most of the people you meet will behave badly because they are insecure, anxious, are naturally aggressive, or have learned that bullying helps them get what they want. Don't make assumptions about the dark triad personality traits. Unless you are their doctor, you are not qualified to diagnose them.

Also most people aren't monsters even if they occasionally act monstrous. All you can really do is focus on the behavior that is problematic. And either work to fix it with behavioral modification techniques, or fire them, or find another job.

~~~~~

CHAPTER 5: BEHAVIORAL SCIENCE ON HOW BEHAVIORS ARE LEARNED AND UNLEARNED

What are these behavioral modification techniques? I'm so glad you asked.

First – the science. We have 70 plus years of behavioral research that shows us the same thing. If we want to extinguish unwanted behavior, we need to pay attention to how the behavior is rewarded and reinforced and how often these rewards occur.

Rewards & Reinforcements

Let's start with rewards and reinforcements. If a behavior is occurring, it's because at some point in the past, it was rewarded and reinforced. If you want it to stop – you need to stop reinforcing it. This sounds simple, but it's tricky to actually do right.

Behavioral reinforcement is like a dance. Person 1 does something, person 2 responds. Person 1 then responds to person 2 and so on. Around it goes. Each person is responding to the behavioral stimulus of the other person.

The key to taking control of this dynamic is to understand your response is triggering responses in the other person. Choose your response wisely and you can get a different outcome.

Stimulus response reinforcement options.

There are 3 possible responses to any given stimulus:

1) Positive - they like what happened and it's pleasurable.

2) Negative – they didn't like it at all or it hurts.

3) Neutral – neither good nor bad.

Not only will we experience one of these three possible responses (positive, negative, or neutral), - our response to our response to what they did – will be experienced by them – either as positive, negative, or neutral as well. We respond to them and they respond to us responding to them.

Controlling the dynamic

So how do we control it? By controlling OUR response and choosing our response wisely.

Understand that if you have an unwanted behavior being directed at you, you do not want to positively reinforce it. At. All. We don't want people behaving badly to learn that it's good to behave badly.

You also don't want to negatively reinforce the behavior. Because negative reinforcement is still reinforcement. What the person will learn is that behaving badly towards you is totally justified because you behaved badly towards them.

And no – it doesn't matter who started it. You are an adult – act like it. Even if the other person isn't in control of their behavior - you be in control of yours.

Your only other option is a neutral response where you don't positively reward them or punish them. They just don't get what they want from you – whatever that is. Think about this as removing the reward.

The great news is that the neutral response is validated by science to work to get unwanted behaviors to stop. You don't remove their reward to punish them. You can do this compassionately and with dignity and it will work. I will get more into exactly how this works later.

Reinforcement Schedules

The next thing to understand about behavioral science is that – how often a person gets a reinforcement or reward impacts their behavior as well. There are two possible reinforcement schedules – consistent and variable.

Consistent is when they get the same response every time. Variable is when sometimes it's positive, sometimes it's negative, sometimes it's neutral. Variable reinforcement actually escalates the unwanted behavior and makes it worse – a lot worse.

What works to get unwanted behavior to stop?

The science is very clear on this. Consistent, neutral response is the only good way to get unwanted behavior to stop. I realize that this is not very satisfying. But it is dignified.

~~~~~

CHAPTER 6: APPLYING THIS TO YOUR BOSS

Ho can you use this information to humanistically handle bad bullying bosses so that you can take control of the dynamic?

First, think about how you might be able to help them and then manage up. Should you ideally have to do this? No, of course not. Is this a part of pretty much every job you will ever have? Yes.

Don't think of this as an imposition on you. You, as a professional dignified person, help others in the workplace be their best. Including your boss. That's what leaders do. So do it. Willingly and with compassion and dignity.

If they are anxious – help them be less anxious. Reassure them. Respond promptly. Let them know they are being heard. Ask how you can help. What do they need?

If they have control issues, help them feel like they are in control. Copy them so they feel like they are in the loop. Make sure you run decisions past them.

Anxiety and control issues are usually just about lack of information. So even when nothing is going on – let them know that. This is about what they need to reduce stress levels so they can be at their best. You are there to help and support them.

Note: This doesn't mean you let them walk all over you. It just means you can often help yourself by helping the other person cope with the uncertainty that happens in the workplace.

For example:

I used to work for a brilliant person. But this person had serious anxiety and control issues. When he first hired me as a remote employee, he left four messages in a 2-hour period before I even started working for him and he had almost convinced himself that I was ghosting him. I wasn't. I was out running errands.

I knew right away that I needed to a) set boundaries for him and b) do a bit of hand-holding to reassure him that everything was going to be ok and c) I had to schedule regular check-in times with him so that his needs to know what was going on were met.

Was this extra work? Yes, of course. It would have been more pleasant to not have to constantly reassure my boss that things were ok. But that's what this boss needed. And it was part of my job to manage my relationship with my boss. So it wasn't a problem.

Once I was able to reinforce his needs while creating the boundaries around my needs, we got along great. As I said, he is a brilliant person. It would have been very easy for me to feel bullied by him. But that wasn't what was happening. He was just anxious and needed reassurance.

My attitude towards him – viewing him with dignity and compassion - is what made our relationship work. I handled a potentially bad bullying boss humanistically.

Are they well intentioned ... or not?

Most bosses are well intentioned - and they respond well to well-intentioned support. My anxious boss responded well and respected the boundaries I set up as long as I kept him informed.

There are some situations, though, that won't be so easily solved. No every boss is well intentioned. Not every boss will respect boundaries. Some are naturally aggressive and habitual bullies.

You may not be able to fix those bosses. You should be able to mitigate their behavior and minimize the harm they are doing, but you won't be able to train them to not be aggressive. Sorry.

And if it turns out they have a dark triad personality trait – you DEFINITELY won't be able to fix them.

I am not saying this to discourage you. I think it's best to be honest. You can't fix a problem unless you understand how to do it and what the realistic limits are.

Some advice

My advice is – assume you have a minor problem - start working to help the boss be better. If they respond well – great. If they don't – keep at it. Keep documenting what is going on and then, if necessary, take employment action or find another job.

~~~~~

CHAPTER 7: HOW TO REMOVE REWARDS OR WORK AROUND A BAD BULLYING BOSS

What should you do if your boss really is a bully and you need to control the dynamic so that a bad bullying boss is no longer rewarded?

First – be dignified and professional. Remember, you do not know at first glance what is really going on or why this person is behaving the way that they are. So don't assume you do. Treat everyone with compassion and dignity – and document everything.

Remember when I told you about my old boss? The way I fixed that was with excessive documentation. I emailed and communicated with him about everything. I did this for 3 reasons:

1. To make sure we were both clear on what expectations were
2. To make sure he wasn't being triggered unnecessarily, and
3. out of compassion.

But again - this approach only really works for the well-meaning but incapable of behaving properly types. If it turns out that you are dealing with one who is intentionally abusive: maintain your professionalism and document everything. And I mean everything.

You may not be able to fix this on your own. And that's ok. If they are your boss, it isn't your job to fix them. All you can do is do your job with dignity and professionalism. If they aren't capable of that – that is on them, not you.

The best you can sometimes hope for is that they get fired or you get another job before you are fired.

Using Documentation as a Tool to Resolve Problems

Ideally, we should first be trying to identify what the problem really is so that it can be fixed. Often, the problem is not what we think it is and our perception of interpersonal relationships may be flawed.

Documenting everything and approaching the situation with dignity and compassion will help with that. It can help resolve these problems and reset frayed relationships.

FOR EXAMPLE:

I volunteer with several groups. I was butting heads with a colleague/leader of one of the groups. I was so annoyed by his behavior. I was actually considering quitting because I really didn't need to be disrespected the way I felt he was disrespecting me.

He was asking for my time, then not telling me what I needed to know to volunteer with him and then getting annoyed with me that I was asking questions he thought were irrelevant. I would spend hours on the phone with him – trying to figure out what he wanted me to do and where he wanted me to be. And when I'd call him to ask for clarification so I could – you know – buy a plane ticket and book a hotel room to be where he wanted me to be, I couldn't even get dates out of him as he would talk about something else entirely.

I felt like he wasn't respecting my time and my time is precious. I blew up and was ready to quit, but the other leaders and colleagues begged me to stay.

To fix this, I treated it as a communication problem. I used a documentation to help fix it. I started cc'ing the other leaders on every communication. I refused to communicate with only him. I always brought someone else in to ensure if there was a disagreement about what we talked about, we had a third party to help us sort it out. I followed up all conversations with emails that cc'd my other colleagues to make sure everyone was on the same page.

The increase in documentation removed any space for misunderstanding and created conditions to correct misunderstandings. I didn't do this to prove that I was right and he was wrong. I did this to remove my own triggers and to remove any rewards I might get from feeling upset and self-righteous.

Notice that I'm talking about fixing my own stimulus response pattern. I tweaked what I was doing to both retrain myself and by extension to reset the stimulus response pattern he and I had fallen into.

The other thing I did was I treated him with dignity and I tried to carry myself with dignity. I didn't blame him. I didn't accuse him of anything. I just started documenting every single conversation. I was still seriously annoyed with him. That took a while to go away. But the documentation helped make sure he and I weren't triggering each other into bad behavior.

The importance of humanistic commitment & compassion

The other thing we did was we started sharing ourselves more. Let me explain what I mean by that. We brought our whole selves to our work. It is very easy in a work environment, even a volunteer environment, to bring only your professional self to the work. We, as a group, decided to share our full selves. Our fears, insecurities, passions, other work, dreams and desires, family situations, and everything.

In other words, we actively and intentionally humanized ourselves and each other. With a goal of supporting one another as humans first and foremost – understanding that we were sometimes going to fail to be our best selves.

And a funny thing happened. The more we learned about each other - the more we liked each other. And the more we saw each other as fully human - the better we started working together. A relationship that had frayed badly is great now. And I genuinely like him as a human being and I adore my colleagues.

Work that was intolerable became enlivening. When we make mistakes in interpersonal dynamics, we can forgive and move forward because social trust is there. We understand each other's intentions as good. We are all committed to treating each other with dignity and listening without being defensive when we make a mistake, and to supporting each other through difficult times.

If someone is going through a difficult time personally, we make space for them and offer our support. That sounds ideal, doesn't it? We created that humanistic workplace culture between us intentionally.

The group, by the way, is the International Humanistic Management Association. We strive to practice what we preach! We also see each other as equal colleagues. We collaborate together. There are no "bosses" in our group. So there is no such thing as a bad bullying boss. Just positive or negative social interactions that we all have the ability to moderate and help support each other through.

What should our goal be?

If a boss is behaving badly, our goal should be to help them learn more prosocial responses and better management behavior. We do this by rewarding the good behavior and not reinforcing the bad behavior, and redirecting them to good behavior. Documentation, compassion, and dignity will help us coach them and ourselves into being better, more effective colleagues.

~~~~~

CHAPTER 8: WHAT IF THEY ARE REALLY ABUSIVE?

If they really are an abusive person – and it's not just a failure to behave well - then our goal should be to help the company get rid of this manager.

We should do this not to harm the bully or to save ourselves; rather we should do this to help the company and our colleagues eliminate a toxic person from our midst. And again – using a documentation approach will help us accomplish this and make it clear what is really going on.

If things fall into this last category, every conversation should be documented. This may seem like overkill, but you are going to need it later and it will help you fix the problem while maintaining your dignity.

Focus on solving the problem ... professionally

You don't start doing this to get them in trouble. You do this to clarify expectations and promises and to make sure that responsibilities are clear. You don't want the problems of the past to prevent proper problem solving in the present. You are being professional. This is how professionals solve these sorts of communication problems.

If they are harassing you with scheduling issues, document all discussions and try and work through it, giving them the benefit of the doubt. But always, always standing your ground and not giving in to the harassment. Your focus should be on fixing the problem. Not on proving that someone else is a problem. They may be. They may not be. If they are, that will reveal itself to everyone without you having to make the case.

If they aren't a problem, your professionalism, compassion, dignity, and focus on problem solving will help make sure the problem is actually solved. Trust me, as emotionally tempting as it is to try and prove your archnemesis is evil, it won't solve the problem. The only thing that will solve the problem – is solving the problem.

When you do this, you will be seen as dignified and professional because you will be. If the other person is not, that will become obvious. You do not need to stoop to their level ever. Let them wallow if that is their choice. Stay above that and focus on problem solving professionally and document everything in an effort to provide clarity to the situation.

Bullies can't hide from documentation

If they are truly bullying you and others, they are going to hate you documenting everything. They may attempt to retaliate. That's fine. That's on them. Don't take it personally even though it is directed at you.

Be prepared for it instead and handle it with dignity and grace. The documentation of their behavior means they can't hide anymore. By documenting everything you are removing the reward because their bullying isn't causing you to acquiesce to them.

That's all YOU need to do and that is easily accomplished by excessive CYA documentation. YOU are giving them the benefit of the doubt that they are well intentioned. If they are well intentioned, they will respond well to your efforts. If they aren't well intentioned, they will reveal themselves through this same process.

Here's why. When a bully loses their reward, they respond by escalating to get their reward back. If they continue to not get their reward, they will escalate more. Smart, strategic people give up quickly. Sabotage isn't as important as not losing their job.

Pathological Escalation

Pathological people will not be able to help themselves. Their behavior will become worse and it will be on full display for everyone to see thanks to the documentation. And again, this is predicted to occur and we have 70 plus years of research to back this up.

If someone is going to blow out spectacularly (meaning they are going to behave stupendously bad), then there is really nothing you can do to stop them. And you really don't need to help them. If they are set on digging a hole that they can't get out of, let them. Don't dig it for them. Instead, feel bad for them.

By staying calm, professional, and treating everyone with dignity and compassion, you can stay above the fray. Focus on problem solving and leave the stupid interpersonal pettiness to those who can't help themselves.

I don't overtly defend myself. I don't think in those terms anyway. When things get bad, I focus on problem solving. Doing that clears away the clutter. It helps me focus on what is important. Other people see that and respond to it positively. And no, this isn't pretty and yes, it's incredibly stressful to go through something like this.

Standing up to retaliating bosses ... with dignity

When a bullying boss can no longer hide, and they become overtly aggressive – it can get NASTY. Because they are a boss, they have the power and ability to retaliate economically and more. Be prepared for that possibility and document everything.

And yes, you could end up losing your job. If you try to stop a bad bullying boss – and it's your bad bullying boss – they have the ability to fire you. But you can still control things and behave with dignity and professionalism and make it hard for them to do this.

I have ended all my jobs on basically good terms and with my dignity intact, even in situations where I was basically fired.

One time I worked for a guy who was incompetent and grossly sexist. He dropped our lead flow down to almost nothing and he would rub himself in front of me. He would lean back in his chair and stroke himself using both hands … in front of me.

I stood up to him when he said something racist to a client in front of me. He was unable to fire me. He had to eliminate my position to justify getting rid of me to top management. I don't have any regrets about how I behaved. Under stress, I behaved consistent with my personal values. I didn't sacrifice my values. Knowing that under stress I am still a good person is priceless.

~~~~~

CHAPTER 9: THE IMPORTANCE OF DIGNITY

Dignity is important.

No one can take your dignity away from you. How you behave is up to you. It is very easy to feel sorry for yourself and to view yourself as a victim. Don't fall into this trap. If the other person is behaving badly, that is their choice. Do not allow them to make you feel like you don't have dignity.

You have dignity – if you choose to act with dignity. It doesn't matter how the other person behaves, you can still choose to act with dignity. Demanding respect isn't something a dignified person does because they don't need their dignity validated by other people.

If you are waiting for someone who is not treating you with dignity to do so – you may be waiting a long time. Don't give people that sort of power over you. If you respond to bad behavior directed at you with professionalism and grace, you will feel dignified. And you will be able to give and get dignity freely.

Dignity is not a finite thing. The more you act with dignity, the more you have. And no one can take your dignity away from you. So go forth and be dignified.

~~~~~

CHAPTER 10: **HUMANISTIC MANAGEMENT AS AN ALTERNATIVE**

This brings me to the topic of humanistic management. To me, this is what we should all be striving towards.

Workplaces would be awesome if leaders and managers were:

- Ethical
- Responsible
- Compassionate

Imagine a workplace where everyone is treated with dignity and as a real human being and not just as a cog in a machine.

When you are faced with a bad bullying boss, you have a choice about how you respond. So ask yourself – who do you want to be?

What I can tell you is – working with people who intentionally strive to be ethical, responsible, compassionate, professional, and dignified - is fulfilling and enlivening.

These sorts of work cultures don't just happen. They have to be intentionally created. And they are created by people choosing to live their ideals.

CHAPTER 11: ABOUT THE AUTHOR

Jennifer Hancock is a mom, author of several books, and founder of Humanist Learning Systems. Jennifer is unique in that she was raised as a freethinker and is considered one of the top speakers and writers in the world of Humanism today. Her professional background is varied including stints in both the for profit and non-profit sectors. She has served as Director of Volunteer Services for the Los Angeles SPCA, sold international franchise licenses for a biotech firm, was the Manager of Acquisition Group Information for a ½ billion-dollar company and served as the executive director for the Humanists of Florida. When she became a mother, she decided to stay at home, but that didn't last long. Shortly after her son was born, she published her first book, *The Humanist Approach to Happiness: Practical Wisdom*. Her speaking and teaching business coalesced into the founding of Humanist Learning Systems which provides online personal and professional development training in humanistic business management and science-based harassment training that actually works.

More Learning from Jennifer Hancock

Other books by Jennifer Hancock

- The Humanist Approach to Happiness
- Jen Hancock's Handy Humanism Handbook
- The Bully Vaccine
- The Humanist Approach to Grief and Grieving
- How to Win Arguments Without Arguing
- Ending Harassment & Retaliation in the Workplace
- Why Bullies Bully & How to Stop Them Using Science
- Reality Based Decision Making for Effective Strategy Development
- Planning for Personal Success

- Why Conflict Management Doesn't Work When the Problem is Bullying
- Why Bullies Bully and How to Stop Them Using Science
- How to Handle Cranky Customer Problems Using Behavioral Science
- How to De-escalate Conflicts Using Behavioral Science
- Bridging the Generation Divide: Millennials vs. Boomers
- How to Talk to Your Child's School About Bullying

Courses taught by Jennifer Hancock

- Workplace Bullying for HR professionals
- Living Made Simpler
- An Introduction to Humanism
- Socratic Jujitsu: How to Win Arguments Without Arguing

- Why Conflict Resolution Doesn't Work When the Problem is Bullying
- Bridging the Generational Divide: Millennials vs. Boomers
- Ending Harassment and Retaliation in the Workplace
- Reality Based Decision Making for Effective Strategy Development
- How to De-escalate Conflicts Using Behavioral Science
- Why is Change so Hard?
- Principles of Humanistic Management
- 7 Sins of Staff Management
- How to Handle Cranky Customer Problems
- New Manager Orientation
- Humanist Group Leadership Lessons
- Sexual harassment training that works – general
- Sexual harassment training that works – AB 1825

- Stop Bullying in our Workplace – Staff Training
- Sexual Harassment Compliance Training
- No Fear Act Training
- Planning for Personal Success!
- Talking to your child about death
- The Bully Vaccine Toolkit
- How to talk to your child's school about bullying
- Why Bullies Bully & How to Stop Them
- How to Prevent Passive-Aggressive People from Wreaking Havoc in the Workplace

Connect with Me Online:

Twitter:
http://twitter.com/#!/JentheHumanist

Facebook:
http://www.facebook.com/JentheHumanist

Or sign up for my mailing list:
http://eepurl.com/c3LuI

~~~~~

The End

######

www.ingramcontent.com/pod-product-compliance
Lightning Source LLC
Chambersburg PA
CBHW070837220526
45466CB00002B/803